FLORENCE
PISA SIENA
SAN GIMIGNANO

THE GEMS OF TUSCANY

Published by
ITALCARDS
bologna Italy

TUSCANY
General notices

Perhaps no other Italian region has such a wealth of natural and artistic treasures as Tuscany has. Sea, Alps and Appenines, verdant pine woods, natural parks and rolling hills, a climate favoured by the combination of many elements which make the spring-time long and the winter short; famous thermal resorts, excellent produce of the land envied all over the world: what more can be said to complete this general description? There is its artistic treasure, not hidden and protected but hung out in the sun, in its splendid towns and cities, in its villages scattered along the Valdarno, in the Val d'Elsa, etc. Which should be remembered first? Florence or Pisa, Arezzo or Siena? Livorno or Lucca and then Grosseto, Massa Carrara, Pistoia? Or Prato, Volterra, Cortona, San Miniato, San Gimignano, Sansepolcro, Pescia, Anghiari ... a list which could go on for ever since even the smallest villages enumerate precious art treasures which tell of a glorious past. Not only the distant past was glorious, but also the not-so-distant past has left unforgettable traces. And if Florence was for a period the capital of Italy, Tuscany can be considered as the centre of the world of art. Or rather, it can be said that Italian art has its natural place of origin here, as does the language.

But Tuscany is not just a region to visit but one to «experience», to stay in for a long time: whith an economy which is prominently agricultural (it is sufficient to remember its vineyards which provide Chianti, the wines of Elba and those of Montepulciano, or the olive trees which give such highly prized oil), it has many other attributes which enrich its sources of living. Rich in minerals (iron from the island of Elba, mercury from Monte Amiata, marble from the Apuan Alps, lignite from Valdarno, etc.), Tuscany also has the industries to work them. Alongside these is a valuable and varied series of craft industries: leather goods, strawwork, embroidery, glass-ware, ceramics, alabaster, metals, wood, cloth: in short, nothing is lacking.

Among the many virtues of the region, we should not forget the good, simple and genuine cooking based on roast meat, game and fish, dressed with the exquisite oil of the region and accompanied by excellent wines. There are also many sweet specialities (biscuits from Prato, «cantucci», castagnacci, panforti, buccellato, «cenci», zuccotti, etc.).

And in conclusion we have the folklore, which in the land of Tuscany is both overwhelming in quantity nad charming. It is sufficient merely to consider the Palio of Siena to explain what the region is capable of (every year, tens of thousands of people watch the two performances on July 2nd and August 16th, with great enthusiasm); but there is practically no city which does not have a yearly festival linked to its traditions and to its history. At Arezzo there is the Saracen's Tournament. at Pistoia that of the Bear; at Lucca the Festival of the Crossbow; at Pisa the Battle of the Bridges and the regatta of the Marine Republics; at Sansepolcro the Festival of the Crossbowmen; at Grosseto the Rose Tournament; not to mention the many Florentine festivals (ball game in costume), the «scoppio del carro» (blowing up of a float), the criket festival and the paper lantern festival, etc,) and those of more recent institution, such as the Carnival of Viareggio.

Among the many festivals, we should not forget the Florentine Music Festival of May, the numerous exibitions of art, antiques, craft industries, cinema and literature which make Tuscany a forge in which the fire never goes out.

FLORENCE

FLORENCE
Historical notices

To find the first traces of civilization in the Arno valley we must go back to the Iron Age.

For many centuries the Etruscans ruled this land until the conquest by the Romans who founded a «Municipium» known as «Florentia».

In spite of the subsequent invasions and terrible ravages suffered, this colony achieved, towards the XI century, a remarkable degree of economic welfare.

It is during this period that the Baptistry, the first architectural masterpiece of the town, was built.

During the following centuries Florence became the cradle of the Renaissance and, moreover, the centre of European civilisation.

This was the result of an encreasing economic power and intellectual and political capacity, its caracteristics along the centuries.

It was, at first, a fief of the Marquises of Tuscany and later on it became the theatre of violent struggles between this ancient noble family and the powerful guild of craftsmen. Cut of this deep rivalry two opposite factions formed: the «Guelfi» partisans of the Pope and the «Ghibellini» partisans of the Emperor.

This internal conflict did not prevent the exceptional cultural political and economic development of Florence which, by the end of the XIII Century had succeeded in spreading its domination over Arezzo, Pistoia and Siena.

In the meantime the masterpieces of Giotto, Cimabue, Arnolfo di Cambio and the great poet Dante flourished.

Characteristic of the XIV Century were, instead, the literary masterpieces of Petrarca and Boccaccio, and the architectural ones of Andrea di Cione known as «Orcagna».

During this period the so called «Tumulto dei Ciompi» took place (1378), a rebellion of the lowest working classes against the richer middle class.

Subsequently the Medici Family with Cosimo the Elder, began to assert and expand its influence; from then on, the Medici would rule over Florence for almost three centuries.

Piero succeeded his father, Cosimo, but it was under Lorenzo, named «Il Magnifico», Cosimo's nephew, and artist, patron of the arts and outstanding politician that Florence reached the hight of its splendour.

The following are the names of the most eminent artists of this period: Brunelleschi, Michelozzo, Masaccio, Beato Angelico, Paolo Uccellom, Filippo Lippi, Botticelli e Donatello and the greatest personalities of the Renaissance, Leonardo and Michelangelo.

After Lorenzo's death, the republicans hostile to the Medici, instigated by a dominican friar, Gerolamo Savonarola, seemed to get the upper hand, but the Medici came back and ruled again, until 1737, when the last of the Medici dynasty, Giangastone, died. Florence, by then a Grand Duchy, was ruled by the Lorraine family until its reunion with the kingdom of Italy of which, in 1865, became the Capital.

Nowadays Florence is a wonderful city spreading along the banks of the Arno surrounded by fertile hills covered with orchards, vine-and olive-groves.

Industry, commerce and handy-crafts are also fluorishing, but it is the fact of being known as a cultural and artistic centre that makes Florence so important.

Innumerable are, in fact, the artistic and cultural events which take place there.

In addition to the University, the Cherubini Academy of Music, the various museums and churches there are in Florence magnificent ancient palaces where concerts and artistic performances are held, attracting many people from all over the world.

GIOTTO'S BELL-TOWER

It is a splendid example of Gothic Florentine architecture for the elegance of its structure, the refined marble panelling and its plastic decoration. The bell-tower was begun in 1334 by Giotto and, after his death, the work was carried on by Andrea Pisano and later completed, in 1359, by Francesco Talenti. It is 84.70 metres high and stands on a base 14.45 metres high; from the terrace at the top, which can be reached by climbing 414 steps, the panorama embraces the whole town and the surrounding hills.

Its structure, supported by four corner pilasters, consists of a base divided into two sectors (the first one was built while Giotto was alive), then there are the two floors by Andrea Pisano and finally the three higher ones built by Talenti (of the latter the first two are perforated by two mullioned windows, the third one by a magnificent pointed three-mullioned window).

Details of panels on the Campanile: the creation of Adam and Eve

The base is decorated with a series of bas-reliefs which have now been substituted by copies (the originals being in the Museum of the Opera del Duomo). In the first sector series the «Creation and Life of Man» is by Andrea Pisano, Nanni di Bartolo and Luca della Robbia and, at least part of it, is from designs by Giotto. In the second sector there are the «Planets», the «Virtues», the «Liberal Arts» and the «Sacraments», executed by pupils of Andrea Pisano and, probably, of Alberto Arnoldi. Above the base one can see the niches which contained 16 statues of «Prophets», «Sybils» and of the «Baptist», the work of Florentine artists of XIV and XV century, among which Donatello; some of these statues have been replaced with copies; the originals are kept in the Museum of the Opera del Duomo.

Giotto's Campanile (1334-1359)

there is the «Madonna with Child», by Arnoldi (1361).

THE DUOMO

It was begun in 1296 by Arnolfo di Cambio on the same ground where the old cathedral of S. Reparata had been, but the work was interrupted when he died (1310) and resumed in 1357, after various vicissitudes and on a much wide scale, by Francesco Talenti who designed the great pillars. Between 1378 when the vault of the central nave was finished and 1421, the work had gone as far as the drum of the dome. It was Brunelleschi who built the dome, between 1420 and 1436, after his daring project had bee accepted, but not without contrasts. The dome was completed with the lantern and the ball at the top as late as 1461.

The façade: The original façade remained unfinished (it was adorned with many statues most of which are now kept in the Museum of the Opera del Duomo), and was demolished in 1587. The present façade has been built on a design by Emilio De Fabris and finished in 1887. Anyway, in spite of the praise-worthy attempt to retrace the original motives of the sides and the apse, the façade does not entirely amalgamate with the ensemble of the building, for lack of authentic stylistic inspiration, even though it has a certain dignity of its own. Of the three bronze doors the left one (1897) and the central one (1903) are the work of A. Passaglia, the right one (1899) of G. Cassioli. The statues and the mosaics on the façade have been made between the end of the XIX and the beginning of the XX century.

In the square in front of the church every year, at Easter, the traditional and famous explosion of the «Carro» takes place, after a dove hase flown from the altar inside the Duomo to the Baptistry.

The interior: It is in the shape of a latin cross divided into three aisles by polistyle pilasters, with high arches and ogival vaults giving it great elegance, while the architectural amplitude in Gothic style induces a sense of severe magnifi-

THE PIAZZA DEL DUOMO

LOGGIA DEL BIGALLO

Built on Gothic Florentine architectural structures, it is ascribed to Alberto Arnoldi (1352-1358) and stands in front of the south door of the Baptistry.

Originally it housed the «Confraternita della Misericordia» which used to show to public charity the abandoned children; then it went to the «Compagnia ospedaliera del Bigallo».

On the side facing the square one can admire the statues of «S.ta Lucy», the «Virgin» and «S. Peter martyr» of the school of Nino Pisano; at a lower level, in the lunette of the door,

Left - from top to bottom: the Bigallo Loggia designed by Alberto Arnolfi (1352-1358); the Cathedral square, the festive «scoppio del Cerro»; *right:* the Cathedral's façade, begun by Arnolfo di Cambio (1296)

Panorama

cence. On the inside of the façade and in the aisles there are, among many others, works by Ghiberti (stained-glass windows), Tino di Camaino, Benedetto da Maiano (busts of Giotto and Squarcialupi), Andrea del Castagno (monument of Nicolò da Tolentino), Paolo Uccello (monument of Giovanni Acuto), Domenico di Michelino (portrait of Dante). The apse is dominated by Brunelleschi's dome, decorated with frescoes by Giorgio Vasari and Federico Zuccari (Last Judgement, 1579) and stained-glass windows made from cartoons by Donatello, Ghiberti, Paolo Uccello and Andrea del Castagno. In the centre of the octagon there is the choir and the high altar (with a «Crucifix» by Benedetto da Maiano) the works of Baccio Bandinelli and Giovanni Bandini. Here is the entrance to the two Sacristies: the «Sacristia Vecchia» on the right, with a terracotta by Luca della Robbia in the lunette of the entrance and, inside, various paintings of XV-XVI century; the «Sacristia Nuova» is on the left, in it Loren-

zo the Magnificient took shelter during the Pazzi Plot (April 26, 1478); it is closed by a bronze gate which has in the lunette above a terracotta, both of them the work of Luca della Robbia. In the central chapel of the apse there is a bronze sarcophagus, the reliquiary of S. Zanobi, a masterpiece by Ghiberti. Finally, in the first chapel of the left apse, there is the «Pietà», an impressive marble sculpture by Michelangelo belonging to the last period of the artist (1550-53).

The Dome: The problem of its building was solved in a daring and antitraditional way by Brunelleschi who raised this dome without any centring. It is 114 metres high including the lantern, and 91 without it, its diameter above the drum is 45.52 metres and it is composed of two shells to give better protection to the inner one and, at the same time, to give a more elegant ogee shape to the outer one. The immense ribs of the dome support and inclose the lantern which has on top a ball with a copper cross, the work of Andrea del Verrocchio.

Left - from top to bottom: **Cathedral - the Dome by Brunelleschi (1420-1461); inside the Dome; the Latin Cross interior with a nave and two aisles;** *right:* **the marble «Pietà» by Michelangelo (1550-1553)**

10

THE BAPTISTERY

Consecrated to St. John the Baptist, patron of the city, it was built in the IIth century on the site of a paloechristian monument, of which there are various remains in the foundation. It was constructed on an octagonal plan, with a double row of arches surmounted by an octagonal pyramid: the cupola of segments, which correspond to the sides of the octagon. It is of Romanesque architecture with decoration in coloured marble. We enter by the south door.

The exterior. The south door, the oldest, is the work of Andrea Pisano (1330): the twenty upper panels show scenes of «St. John the Baptist». The eight below, «The Theological and Cardinal Virtues». Particularly worthy of attention are «The Banquet of Herod», «The funeral of the Saint» and «Hope». The door jambs are by Vittorio Ghiberti, the son of Lorenzo (1462), the three statues above the portal: «The Baptist between Salome and the Executioner» by Vincenzo Danti (1571).

North door. The first of the two carried out by Ghiberti, who was entrusted with the work after the famous competition in which Brunelleschi took part. The twenty upper panels show «Scenes from the New Testament», the other eight lower panels show «The

Left - from top to bottom: the Baptistry (Church of St. John the Baptist) 11th century?; the South Door by Andrea Pisano (1330); the North Door by Lorenzo Ghiberti (1403-1424); *right:* the so-called «Paradise» bronze door by Lorenzo Ghiberti (1378-1455)

12

Evangelist» and «The Teachers of the Church». In the panels of this door, we see the late gothic style to which the artist was tied, by tradition. Above the portal statues of «The Baptist between the Levite and the Pharisee», the work of Gio. F. Rustici (1511).

East door (opposite the cathedral). Considered to be Ghiberti's masterpiece (1452), Michelangelo defined it as «the door of Paradise». In the ten gilded bronze panels, Ghiberti under the influence of Donatello, shows scenes of the old Testament, with pictorial and perspective reliefs, of excellent workmanship.

Interior. Large octagonal vase, with walls covered in marble, and a cupola decorate with mosaics, important testimony 12th century pictorial art, showing the direction of the Romanesque current in Florence. The mosaics were certainly begun by Maestro Jacopo in 1225. They show; in the tribune: at the centre of the vault «The Mystic Angel», on the right «The Madonna and Child», on the left «The Baptist Enthroned». On the left of the cupola: «The Universal Judgement» dominated by a large figure of Christ; inside the lantern «The Heavenly Orders». In the remaining parts of the vault, which is the work of Venetian and Florentine artists including Cimabue, from top to bottom: 1. «Scenes from Genesis up to the Flood», 2. «The Story of Joseph», 3. «The Story of Mary and Jesus», 4. «The Story of John the Baptist». (The vault can be illuminated on request). The baptismal font is the work of the Pisana school (1371). The floor, inlaid with signs of the zodiac and of oriental motifs, is of 1209. Along the wall we notice, on the rigth side of the tribune, the tomb of the Antipope John XXIII by Donatello and Michelozzo (1422-1427). There follows a tomb slab of Bishop Ranieri (12th century). On the left of the tribune, between the two Roman Sarcophagi: the beautiful «Magdelene», a wooden sculpture by Donatello (1371).

Left - from top to bottom: **the Interior of the Baptistry; Byzantine mosiacs in the Baptistry dome (14th century);** *right - from top to bottom:* **Donatello's «Cantoria» (1403-1439); the «Cantoria» by Luca della Robbia: details showing figures of children dancing and playing instruments (1431-1438); Donatello's «Habakkuk», nicknamed «Zuccone» (vegetable marrow).**

MUSEUM OF THE OPERA DEL DUOMO

Here are kept the works of art from the Duomo, the Bell-tower and the Baptistry. Its main point of interest is the XIV and XV century Florentine sculpture. The hall of the old façade of the Duomo contains, amont other works, some «Virgins», «Santa Reparata» and the «Statue of Boniface VIII» by Arnolfo di Cambio, «St. John» by Donatello and «St. Luke» by Nanni di Banco; in the adjoining rooms there are some architectural fragments, illuminated codices and jewellery. On the upper floor are kept the two famous «Cantorie» (choirs) by Luca della Robbia and Donatello which, in the past, had been in the octagon of the dome in the Duomo. In the same room are shown

the 16 statues from the niches of the Bell-tower, the work of Andrea Pisano, Nanni di Bartolo and Donatello (of the latter one should remember «Habbakuk» and «Abraham and Isaac»). In the following rooms there are the panels from the Bell-tower, the work of Andrea Pisano, Luca della Robbia, Alberto Arnoldi and others; finally there is the well-known «altar of the Baptistry» an exceptional work of jewellers' art which took over 114 years to create.

THE PIAZZA DELLA SIGNORIA

This great square for many centuries has been the focal point of Florentine political and civic life; it is, together with its monuments and the works of art, one of the most important architectural open areas of the city and its unparralleled charm has remained untouched throughout the centuries. Many events of great interest such as the «Flower Show» and the traditional «Foot-ball match» in XVI century costume, still take place there.

This colourful scene is dominated by the imposing «Palazzo Vecchio» and by the «Loggia della Signoria».

On the left of the Palazzo there is a fountain, the «Fonte di Piazza», the work of Bartolomeo Ammannati and his pupils (1563-1575), commissioned by Cosimo I, with the gigantic statue of Neptun, nick-namek by the Florentines «Biancone» because of its white ungraceful shape. On the contrary the statues adorning the basin are of a higher artistic value.

Towards the centre of the square a porphyry plaque marks the spot where Gerolamo Savonarola and his followers were hanged and burnt on May 23, 1498.

On the left of the Fountain is an equestrian monument to Cosimo I de' Medici by Giambologna (1594). The three bas-reliefs of the pedestal illustrate episodes of Cosimo's life. At the end of the Piazza one can see the Tribunale della Mercanzia (XIV century) bearing on its façade the escutcheons of the Florentine Guilds, and the Palazzo Uguccioni which was built by Mariotto di Zanobi Folfi in 1549.

In addition to the innumerable historical works of art the Piazza contains also the Palazzo della Cassa di Risparmio where one can visit the Raccolta della Regione, a rich collection of contemporary Italian paintings and sculptures, which was given to the city of Florences as a donation in 1970. Works by famous painters such as Birolli, Campigli, Carrà, Casorati, Cassinari, De Chirico, De Pisis, Guttuso, Licini, Maccari, Mafai, Morandi, Menzio, Morlotti, Rosai, Scipioni, Nedova, and by sculptors such as Broggini, Fontana, Manzù, Marino, Martini, Mirko

Piazza della Signoria - *Left:* **Palazzo Vecchio;** *below:* **the Fountain of Neptune by B. Ammannati (1563-1575)**

are on display in different rooms on the two floors of the gallery.

On the left of the steps leading to the entrance to Palazzo Vecchio is the «Marzocco», a copy of Donatello's marble lion (now at the Museo Nazionale) holding the armorial bearings of the City of Florence an a XV century pedestal; and «Judith and Holopherne», a dramatic bronze also by Donatello (1455-60). In front of the portal is a copy of Michelangelo's «David» (now at the Galleria dell'Accademia) and «Hercules and Cacus» a mediocre marble group by Baccio Bandinelli (1533).

Above the portal is a frieze bearing Christ's monogram between gilded lions.

Piazza della Signoria - *above left:* **Judith and Holophernes by Donatello (1455-1460);** *below, on the right:* **View from the Signoria Loggia, the work of Benci di Cione and Simone Talenti (1376-1381)**

THE LOGGIA DELLA SIGNORIA

It is also called Loggia dei Lanzi after the Granducal Lansquenet Guard (XVI century) or Loggia dell'Orcagna after the homonymous artist to whom it was wrongly attributed. Built by Benci di Cione and Simone Talenti between 1376 and 1381 in late Florentine Gothic style it was intended for the ceremonials of the Signoria — among which the elections of both the Gonfalonier and the Priors. Above the piers of its open hall are some framed sculptures by Florentine artists of the late XIV century: the four Cardinal Virtues (Fortitude, Temperance, Justice and Prudence) on the side of the Piazza; and the three Theological Virtues (Faith, Hope and Charity) on the side facing the Uffizi. Under the Loggia are a number of sculptures by outstanding artists of different periods. The famous «Perseus» by Cellini is on the parapet of the Loggia on the left: the Greek mythology hero is represented while lifting the head of the decapitated Medusa whom — according to the legend — he slew using his polished shield as a reflecting mirror in order to avoid being petrified by the monster's look. From the blood abundantly spilled by the hacked off neck of Medusa — the legend goes on — two children were born — Crisaore and Pegasus. In the well-wrought pedestal of the statue are carved four niches containing four sculptures (Jove, Minerva, Mercurius and Danae with the child Perseus). Under the niches is a bas-relief representing Perseus liberating Andromeda. They are copies of sculptures now at the Museo Nazionale (Bargello).

On the front right-hand side of the Loggia in the «Ratto delle Sabine», a masterpiece sculpture by Giambologna (1583). The group is shaped in such a way as to recall a piramid and to allow a symbolic interpretation according to which the three ages of man are represented — old age at the foot, maturity in the middle, and youth at the top.

On both sides of the steps leading to the Loggia are two lions made of marble — the one on the right is the more ancient and dates back to the classical age, whereas the one on the left is a copy of this one and was made by Flaminio Vacca (1600). In the second row starting from the left is the «Ratto di Polissena» by Pio Fedi (1866). It is followed by two groups, one representing Menelaus holding Patroclus's body (a restored Roman copy of a IV-century-B.C. Greek sculpture) and the other representing Hercules and the Centaur Nessus by Giambologna. At the end of the Loggia are six Roman women, all of the Imperial era with the exception of the third one starting from the left, which has been identified as a portrait of Tusnelda or Germania.

19

Left: **Perseus with the head of the Medusa by Benvenuto Cellini (1554);** *above:* **Menelaus supporting Patroclus (4th century B.C.); the Rape of the Sabine by Giambologna (1583)**

Palazzo Vecchio - Michelozzo's Courtyard (1470)

HIS LORDSHIP'S PALACE

Until the 16th century the palace was the seat of the Governors, subsequently the home of Cosimo I dei Medici; from 1865-1871 the House of Deputies of the Kingdom of Italy had it's first sittings here; it was also the home of the Ministery of Foreign Affairs; since 1872 it has been the seat of the Municipio.

Interior: We enter the courtyard, restored and renovated by Michelozzo in 1453, richly decorated with stuccos and pictures depicting the marriage of Francesco dei Medici to Giovanna of Austria. In the middle a fountain with the bowl in poryphry and above it a beautiful bronze «Dolphin and Putto» by Andrea del Verrocchio (the original is preserved inside). In the niche above the door «Sampson and philistine» by Pierino da Vinci; on the left side of the courtyard the Arms Room, one of the few remaining parte of the 13th century building. Between this courtyard and the second, which has

pillars by Cronaca, the Vasari staircase taking us to the upper floors and the Monumental Appartments.

The salone dei Cinquecento: (Hall of the Five hundred). Built by Cronaca (1495) for the assemblies of the General Council of the People, after the second expulsion of the Medici, was to have been frescoed by Leonardo and Michelangelo (who only sketched the cartoons later destroyed). The enormous hall was instead decorated and frescoed by Vasari and his school.

The panels of the ceiling tell the «stories of Florence and the Medici» with, in the centre, the «Triumph of Cosimo I». On the entrance wall there is, from the left: «Cosimo is made Duke of Florence by the Senate», a painting on slate by the Ligozzi; the «Defeat of the Pisani at torre S. Vincenzo», «Massimiliano attempts the capture of Livorno», «The assault to Pisa», all of them frescoes by Vasari and his pupils.

On the opposite wall there is: the «Capture of Siena», the «Capture of Porto Ercole», the

«Victory of Marciano», again by Vasari and his school; then «Cosimo founds the order of S. Stefano», a painting on slate by Passignano.

On these two walls are also hung the beautiful tapestries of the Medicean fabric showing the «stories of the Baptist», the work of P. Fevère from cartoons by A. Melissi (XVII century); and, finally, there are six marble groups with the «Labours of Hercules» by Vincenzo de' Rossi.

Left - from top to bottom: **Palazzo Vecchio - the Sala dei Cinquecento, built by Cronaca (1495); Hercules and Diomedes by Vincenzo de' Rossi; the Genius of Victory, from the marble group carved by Michelangelo (1532-34);** *right:* **the Uffizi Palace and Palazzo Vecchio**

THE UFFIZI GALLERY

The building which houses one of the world's most famous art galleries (certainly the most important in Italy) and the «Archivio di Stato» (Record Office) was begun in 1560 by Vasari in late-Renaissance style, and completed in 1580 by Alfonso Parigi and Bernardo Buontalenti according to Vasari's project. This enormous building, devised by order of Cosimo I to contain the administrative offices and the archives of the Florentine State, flanks tghe long square with a portico interrupted by a wide arch with a view of the Arno. After every second column of the portico there is a pilaster with a niche containing a statue of outstanding Tuscan personalities, from Dante to Petrarca, from Leonardo to Michelangelo, from Cosimo to Lorenzo il Magnifico. The gallery offers and unparalleled and complete collection of Florentine and Tuscan painting, and also contains many works of other Italian schools (the most reprented is the Venetian one), a group of Flemish paintings, extremely important because of the influence they had on Italian painting, the famous collection of self-portraits and a great number of ancient sculptures (some of them of great importance like the «Venus of the Medici» of the I century B.C., derived from Prassiteles, or the «Knife-grinder», the «Wrestlers» and «Dionysus and the Satyr»).

In the gallery can also be found a good collection of tapestries, and a «Cabinet of Drawings and Prints», with more than one hundred thousand pieces.

The focal point of the gallery is the Medici and Lorraine collection.

23

Left: the Madonna in Glory, by Giotto; *from top to bottom:* **Madonna and Child, by Fra' Filippo Lippi; Federico da Montefeltro and Battista Sforza, by Piero della Francesca ; Tiziano's Venus**

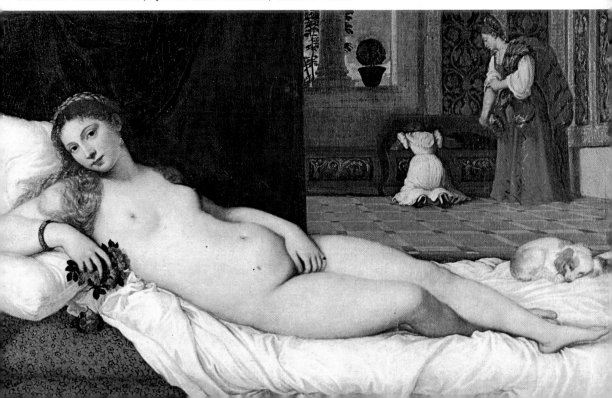

The Birth of Venus and details by Sandro Botticelli

The Holy Family, by Michelangelo

The Annunciation, by Leonardo da Vinci

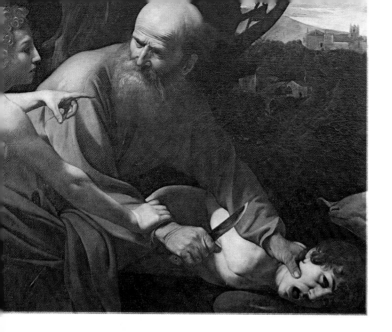

From top to bottom beginning from the left: **the Sacrifice of Isaac, by Caravaggio; the Madonna of the Cardellino, by Raffaello Sanzio; the Head of a Young Girl by Leonardo da Vinci; the Young Bacchus and the Medusa, by Caravaggio**

Top: **the Loggia of the New Market, by Giovanni Battista del Tasso (1547-1551);** *bottom:* **the «Porcellino» (sucking pig), a bronze work by Pietro Tacca (1612)**

Above: **the Pitti Palace, begun by Luca Fancelli in 1457 to a design by Filippo Brunelleschi;** *right:* **Portrait of an Anonimous Subject by Titian**

THE PITTI PALACE

It was begun after 1457 by Luca Fancelli on a project that Filippo Brunelleschi had made in 1440 for Luca Pitti, a rich merchant who was a friend and later a rival of the Medici; this imposing palace, with boldly rusticated masonry, stands on the slope of the Boboli hill and was conceived with rigid geometrical proportions which were fortunately respected in the subsequent additions.

It consists of a ground floor with three doors alternating with four rectangular windows, and two upper-floors, each of them with a balcony connecting seven French windows; after a period when the works were interrupted and the palace sold to the Medici, from 1558 it was enlarged, first by Ammannati who inserted two windows where the side doors had been and built the inner courtyard. Later on Giulio Parigi (1620) added three windows to each side, and his son Alfonso (1640), with additions to the ground-floor and the first floor, brought the façade to its present aspect.

Finally, the two wings, called «rondò», were added during the second half of the XVIII century on a project by Giuseppe Ruggieri. The main door leads into the Ammannati courtyard, flanked on three sides by the inner façade and the wings and on the fourth side by the terrace which looks onto the Boboli gardens (in the central arcade is the XVII century «Grotto of Moses» and, at ground level, the «Fountain of the artichoke», the work of Francesco del Tadda and Francesco Susini).

The palace was first the residence of the Medici and later of the Lorraine, then, in 1860, it went to the Savoy royal family who lived there during the years when Florence was the capital of Italy (1864-71).

At present it houses the Palatina Gallery the «Gallery of Modern Art», the «Silver Museum» and the «Museum of Carriages». It is also possible to visit the «old royal apartments».

The Palatina Gallery's works of art are still arranged following a XVII century pattern and, therefore, a rather elaborate and decorative setting. It contains one of the most renowned and

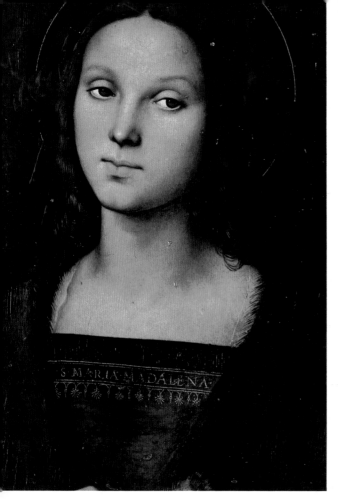

important collections and it is divided into many rooms; here mention is only made of the ones where really exceptional works are exhibited.

After climbing the main staircase and through the Vestibule, the little staircase of the Porphyry Cup, is the following suite of rooms:

Room I: «Iliad»: works by Raffaello, Ghirlandaio, Del Sarto, Tiziano, Velasquez, Bartolini.

Room II: «Saturn»: works by Raffaello, Doni, Perugino, Ghirlandaio, Del Sarto.

Room III: «Jupiter»: works by Del Sarto, Fra Bartolomeo, Raffaello, Bellini.

Room IV: «Mars»: works by Rubens, Murillo, Veronese, Tiziano, Tintoretto, Van Dyck.

Room V: «Apollo»: works by Tiziano, Tintoretto, Rubens, Andrea del Sarto.

Room VI: «Venus»: works by Tiziano and Rubens.

Room VII: «Castagnoli»: decorated by Castagnoli a painter of the XIX Century.

Room VIII: «Suite of the Allegories by Volterrano».

Room IX: Of Fine Art or of Cigoli.

Room X: «Hercules»; Sèvres vase.

Room XI: «Dawn»: works by Empoli and Lorenzo Lippi.

Room XII: «Berenice»: works by Salvator Rosa.

Room XVIII: «Drums»: it derives its name from the shape of the little pieces of furniture. Here is the well-known «St. Sebastian» by Sodoma.

Room XIX: «Prometheus»: works by Signorelli, Filippi and Giulio Romano.

Room XX: «Procetti Gallery»: it bears the name of the painter who decorated it.

Room XXI: «Corridor of the little columns»: Flemish paintings.

Room XXII: «Justice»: works by Tintoretto, Tiziano and Veronese.

Room XXIII: «Flora»: works by Canova, Andrea del Sarto and Pontormo.

Room XXIV: «Putti»: marine landscapes, flowers, fruits, hunting scenes by Rachel Ruysch and Henry Gubbels.

Room XXV: «Ulysses»: works by Raffaello, Tintoretto, Cigoli and Dolci.

Room XXVI: «Bath»: neoclassical style.
Room XXVII: «Education of Jupiter»: works by Caravaggio and Allori.
Room XXVIII: «Stove»: the frescoes on the walls are by Pietro da Cortona.

Off the Venus Room are the State Apartments.

Room I «Niches»; Room II «Green Room»; Room III «Throne Room»; Room IV «Blue Room»; Room V «Baroque Chapel»; Room VI «Parrots»; Room VII «Yellow Room»; Room VIII «Bedroom»; then the suite of rooms of Queen Margherita and the apartment of King Umberto.

On the ground floor of the palace there is the Silver Museum, with collections of goldsmith's art, precious stones, cameos, fabrics, carpets, china and other objects of great value.

On the second floor there is the Modern Art Gallery.

On the ground-floor, by requesting the keeper, it is possible to visit the Museum of historic carriages which is very interesting.

From left to right: **Magdalen, by Perugino (1495), situated in the Sala di Saturno; the Sala dell'Iliade (of the Illiad) with a ceiling decorated by Luigi Sabatelli (1819) with themes taken from Homer's epic poem; Portrait of Cardinal Inghirani (1514) by Raffaello Sanzio (Sala di Saturno)**

Above: **Piazza of Saints Annunziata and Spedale degli Innocenti;** *below:* **the Church of the Holy Spirit, begun by Brunelleschi (1444)**

Above: the Church of Santa Maria Novella, begun in 1246 by the Domenican friars Sextus and Ristoro; *below:* the Church of San Miniato al Monte (1018-1200)

MEDICI CHAPELS

The octagonal Princes Chapel, has a dome designed by Giovanni de' Medici and executed by Matteo Nigetti.

Inside, the walls are covered with marble, golden bronzes and semi-precious stones worked with exceptional skill.

In the New Sacristy, the work of Michelangelo, there are three famous tombs, but only two have been completed.

The one on the left of the entrance is the tomb of Lorenzo, duke of Urbino, the nephew of Lorenzo the Magnificent.

The Duke is represented in a pensive attitude, with two figures on the tomb symbolising Dawn and Dusk.

Opposite is the tomb of Giuliano, Duke of Nemours; he is seated and in armour, at his feet two symbolic figures, Day and Night.

On the right wall the unfinished monument for Lorenzo the Magnificent and his brother Giuliano.

Also by Michelangelo is the statue of the Virgin with Child.

Above: **the Medici Chapels - construction begun in 1604 by Matteo Negretti;** *below:* **the Sepulchral Chapel of the Medici Princes**

Above: **Via Calzaioli and the Church of Orsanmichele (1337);** *below, from left to right:* **the Arte della Lana Palace (1300); the Synagogue (1872-1874)**

GALLERIA DELL'ACCADEMIA

The entrance to the gallery is in Via Ricasoli along the arcades of the Academy of Fine Arts.

The wide and solemn lobby is decorated with Flemish Tapestries of the XVI Century, all of them showing stories of Genesis.

In the Gallery there are scultpures by Michelangelo and paintings of the Tuscan school.

In the first room are the four statues of the «Captives» made by Michelangelo for the tomb of Pope Julius II in Rome.

Towards the end of the room, on the right, is the «Pietà Palestrina» from the chapel in the Church of Palestrina.

Below the dome of the Gallery, is the splendid masterpiece of Michelangelo's juvenile period, «David».

This statue, begun in 1501 was finished three years later.

Formerly placed at the entrance of Palazzo Vecchio, it was subsequently moved to the Academy Gallery.

Left: **a detail from Michelangelo's David;** *below:* **the Tribune and the sculture of David;** *right:* **Michelangelo's David**

THE «BARGELLO»

Towards the end of the XVI Century this palace became the seat of the «Capitano di Giustizia» called «Bargello» and the name remained thereafter. It is the most important civic building after the «Palazzo della Signoria».

Now it houses the National Museum which is extremely interesting for the appreciacion of Tuscan sculpture from XIV to XVII Century.

These are the most important rooms: Armoury - General Council - Porcelain - Ivory - Cellini Room - Little bronzes - Della Robbia Room - Verrocchio - Fireplace.

The courtyard is the most impressive feature of the palace. On three sides it is surrounded by a portico and on the fourth side the beautiful staircase, by Neri di Fioravante, leads to a balcony.

In the centre of the courtyard is the well, used in the past for capital punishment.

Under the portico are displayed several beautiful sculptures.

Above: **the Bargello (1255), the most important public building of the medieval city after the Palazzo Vecchio;** *below - from left to right:* **David by Donatello (1531), the Drunken Bacchus, by Buonarroti (1497-1499); Mercury, by Giambologna**

The Church of St. Lawrence, begun in 1419 by Brunelleschi; *bottom:* the Church of St. Lawrence: the Cloister

BASILICA OF SAN LORENZO

The church of S. Lorenzo is situated in the square of the same name where there is also a picturesque market.

This church is a very ancient one and was built above another one, consecrated in 393 by St. Ambrogio Bishop of Milan.

It was built, the first time, in pre-Romanesque style (c. 1000 A.D.) and rebuilt, from 1421 in its present form by Filippo Brunelleschi to the order of Giovanni di Bicci de' Medici.

The interior has three aisles separated by Corinthian columns. The two pulpits underneath the last two spans of the central nave are by Donatello.

At the foot of the high altar three bronze gratings mark the place in which Cosimo the Elder, called «Pater patriae», was buried. The Old Sacristy, conceived by Brunelleschi, houses important works by Donatello and Andrea Cavalcanti; underneath the archway, on the left, is a bronze and porphyry sarcophagus by Verrocchio.

43

BASILICA OF SANTA CROCE

It faces the square of Santa Croce which, on the other sides, is lined by old palaces.

In this square, during the Medici period, first the tournements took place and later foot-ball matches.

The church belongs to the Franciscans and was built towards 1295, according to plans by Arnolfo di Cambio.

The façade is a modern one (1863) and so is the bell-tower (1865) built in gothic style.

The interior, in the shape of an Egyptian cross is divided into three aisles by octagonal pillars supporting pointed arches.

The main nave has an open-beam roof while the choir and the chapels in the transept have vaulted roofs.

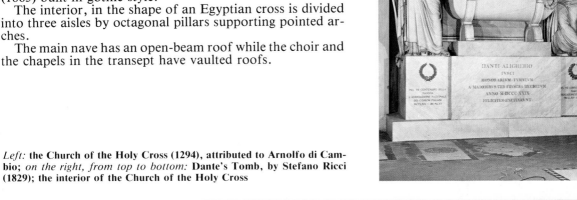

Left: the Church of the Holy Cross (1294), attributed to Arnolfo di Cambio; *on the right, from top to bottom:* Dante's Tomb, by Stefano Ricci (1829); the interior of the Church of the Holy Cross

Below: a view of Piazzale Michelangelo, by night

MUSEUM OF SAN MARCO

It is in the monastery of St. Mark also built by Michelozzo for the Dominicans of Fiesole by the order of Cosimo the Elder.

Among these Dominicans there was Fra Giovanni, named the «Angelico» because of the intense spirituality of his paintings.

Through the cloister of St. Antonino with frescoes by the Angelico can be reached the Chapter House and the hall of the Pilgrims Hospital.

Amongst the most impressive works by the Angelico are «The flight into Egypt» and «The Annunciation».

Above: **St. Mark's Square with its church of the same name;** *below:* **the Annunciation by Fra' Angelico**

PISA

PISA
Its history

Pisa is divided in two parts by the Arno River. It is at 4 mts above sea-level and located on a fertile plain that extends from the foot of the Pisan Mountains to the sea-coast, which is not more than 10 Kms from the town-center. With a population just over one hundred thousand inhabitants Pisa has a military and civil airport, with international landing-place, is an archiepiscopal seat and also boasts a university centre of ancient historical and cultural traditions. The university of Pisa was already active in the twelfth century and is, therefore, one of the oldest, and also one of the most glorious, Italian universities. It is also a main station on the Rome-Genoa railway line with branches to Empoli-Florence and Siena, as well as on another line, to Lucca-Montecatini Terme-Florence. It is a junction of main and toll-roads. That is the reason why from the town the numerous resorts on the Tyrrhenian Sea and in the mountains are easily accessible. The centres for thermal cures are also within an easy reach: S. Giuliano Terme at only 4 Kms, Montecatini and Monsummano Terme at not more than 38-45 Kms.

Regarding the climate that of Pisa can be classified within the most temperate zones of Italy, because the Pisan Mountains, the mountains of «Garfagnana» and the Apuan Alps shelter it from the cold north winds, while the nearby seafront allows it to breathe the temperate west and south winds. As such the town is suitable for a pleasant stay, backed up by a first rate hotel organization and by the opportunity of having within a short range the many spots above mentioned as well as other such as Lucca, Torre del Lago Puccini (with the country-house of the great composer), Collodi with its historical garden, Leghorn, etc., for rich experiences and pleasure trips.

But the town is principally glorified for its ancient and noble past; it is said that Pisa is older than Rome and that it was one of the most powerful marine Republics.

Opinions about its origin are discordant, but the most reliable sources give us to think that most likely it rose between the 5th and the 7th century B.C. At first it was a Greek colony, afterwards an Etruscan one. In 180 B.C. it became a Roman colony named «Colonia Julia Pisana». The fortune of the town was always governed by the sea, that in this period was at the gates of Pisa. In the 11th century Pisa became a powerful marine Republic. That is to say from the period when it was allied with the Romans up to the second Punic war and afterwards when Caesar Octavian established the harbour in a natural bay (the «Sinus Pisanus») and precisely at the estuary of the Arno River where big ships could dock. Up to that time, it had been under Odoacer, the Ostrogothics, the Byzantines, the Longobards and the Franks and then annexed in the Marquisate of Tuscany under the Carolingians.

As a powerful marine Republic, Pisa fought against the Saracens and conquered Corsica, Sardinia and the Balearic Islands; it asserted its high prestige also in the East especially after participating in the 1st Crusade. The problem now was to consolidate and to maintain its influence over the conquered territories and in this intention long and fierce struggles against Amalfi and Genoa for supremacy over land and sea were never lacking. Added to this constant military effort there was strong internal unrest mainly caused by the Guelph-Tuscan league on account of speculations, of contrast on how the enormous amassed wealth was to be administrated. The result was, that even though they managed resist to the Guelph-Free cities and the followers of the Guelphs amongst the citizens of Pisa, the town became slowly weaker, so much so that being engaged contemporaneously on the seas of Levant, in rivalry with the Republic of Venice, and on the Mediterranean against Genoa, it suffered a disastrous defeat by Genoa in the famous battle of Meloria in 1284. It was the «day of Saint Sistus», anniversary of many victories, but this time Pisa had lost. The Republic went on, but the glory, prestige and rule over the sea came to an end. In this manner, after an extraordinary ad-

Aerial View.

venture, the economical and political decline of Pisa started; the free-city institutes broke down and in their place the families of nobles asserted their authority: first the Uguccione della Faggiola, then the Della Gherardesca and later the family Gambacorti. Finally the family D'Appiano ruled over the fortune of Pisa until it passed over to Visconti who ceded it to the authority of Florence in the year 1405.

Although Pisa had now lost its political indipendence, under the wise rule of Medici the town developed progressively as a cultural and intellectual centre. Cosimo the 1st de' Medici, for instance, renewed the study of the Sapienza. Leopoldo the 2nd reorganized the Scuola Normale Superiore founded by Napoleon in the year 1810.

After so many historical vicissitudes, in the year 1860 Pisa joined the Kingdom of Italy with a solemn plebiscite.

During the 2nd World War the town was subjected to notable destruction both from heavy bombing raids and because of the dogged resistance of the Germans on the northern banks of the Arno River, just within the limits of town-walls. This resistance lasted 40 days. Casualties were very high and the destruction was not limited only to public property but also to artistic treasures. In the field of art the famous «Camposanto Monumentale» (Monumental cemetery), the marble walls of which close off the imposing «Piazza dei Miracoli» to the north, was seriously damaged.

CATHEDRAL SQUARE

The monuments which transform a common name of square into the «Piazza dei Miracoli» are: the CATHEDRAL, the BAPTISTRY, the BELL or LEANING TOWER and the MONUMENTAL CEMETERY. A combination of works of architecture and sculpture which rise stately and austere, but at the same time refined and full of charm, placed around a wide tender green lawn. It is in this natural semplicity that

49

the white marbles, so highly worked and rendered precious by human genius, have found a perfect setting. It is exactly in this pleasant simplicity of the «LAWN» that the greatness of the works, which almost seem a creation of nature itself, is wonderfully blended, so much so that the tourist, even if passing hastily by can't help feeling a strong sense of admiration and emotion. This wonderful architectural composition, with so much harmony of styles and colours, contrasts its beauty with that of the ancient walls facing west and east, as well as the building of the 13th century facing south, today seat of the «Spedali Riuniti di S. Chiara».

All this architectonic magnificence of the marbles, the green of the lawn, the ancient walls with their embattlements, the sombre and solemn row of cypresses, form a whole really great, even touching at every hour of the day. In the evening the sight is perhaps even more beautiful be-

cause as the sun sets a dim and soft illumination substitutes its light, rendering the play of lights more suggestive and penetrating.

THE CATHEDRAL

This grandiose architectonic masterpiece in Romanesque-Pisan style was started in the year 1063 by the great architect BUSCHETTO. It is, therefore, the first work undertaken on the spot

that became later the «Piazza dei Miracoli». It was possible because of the enormous wealth amassed by the powerful Sea Republic which at that time Pisa was, particularly after a fruitful excursion on Palermo. The Cathedral was consecrated in the year 1118, even though still incomplete, by Pope Gelasio the 2nd. It was terminated in the 13th century with the erection of the façade, unchanged up to today, by RAINALDO.

The Cathedral, designed in the form of a Latin cross, basically has a romanesque architectural style, but at the same time interprets and absorbs elements of the styles of various periods, thus forming a unique style which has something of sublime. The Cathedral was adorned, a little at the time through the years, with numerous works of art. GIOVANNI PISANO is certainly the artist who excels in these works, especially because he has given us the famous, extremely rich and ingenious PERGAMO (Pulpit).

For a brief idea of its dimensions, the Cathedral is about one hundred meters long. The façade is 35.40 mts wide. It is 34.20 mts high; hence both imposing and of an ingenious and grandiose conception.

The Façade of the Cathedral

The façade of the cathedral is articulated in five orders of arches, the lowest of which has seven blind arches, two lateral and one central gate, separated by columns and pilasters. In the year 1595 a furious fire broke out and destroyed these gates (as well as the ceiling and other works on the inside) hence the gates of today are not the original ones of the master BONANNO, but those made by the artists of the school of Giambologna, i.e. Francavilla, Mocchi and Tacca.

In the central gate is the representation of the life of «Maria». The two lateral ones represent the life of the Redeemer. Still in this inferior order walls are not lacking of numerous tarsia-rose-windows, groves, inlays of ornamental glass and geometrical panels which give a sense of grace and refinement.

The superior orders present open-galleries that contrast with the walls giving depth and movement so much so that the massive proportions of the whole façade become refined, and, at the same time, rendered precious by a minute and elaborate fretwork.

Above the central gate, there is a memorial inscription by Rainaldo. The sarcophagus of BUSCHETTO, who started the construction of the cathedral, lays in the first arcade to the left.

Piazza of the Miracles (dei Miracoli) - harmony, balance and colour.

The façade of the Cathedral.

On the top of the façade, there is a statue of the Madonna by Andrea Pisano and, at the sides, angels of the School of Giovanni Pisano. At both sides of the first order of galleries there are the statues of two evangelists. The whole cathedral, both on the two sides and in the apses, repeats the decorative and ornamental themes of the façade, even if with slight differences. Here decorations are repeated as polychrome tarsias, groved panels, inlays of coloured glass. The whole cathedral is a wonderful work of architecture and sculpture not at all lacking in grace in spite of its stately and massive conception.

The oval-shaped dome shows influences from the Islamic art and is located at the intersection of the transept with the central body of the temple.

The cupola

The cupola of the Cathedral is particularly interesting for its elliptical form. It was added in 1380 during the flowering of the gothic period by Lupo of Gante and Puccio of Gadduccio. The

The nave of Cathedral.

cupola rests on an octagonal drum. The light and dignified gothic gallery which surrounds it does not contrast unfavourably on the stylistic level with the Romanesque complex underneath.

Passing the Baptistry, the Italian gothic demonstrates its very presence, even if timidly, in the harmonious lines of the Cathedral.

Interior of the Cathedral

In order to enjoy all the majesty of the temple, before stopping here and there, we advise you to go to the inner wall of the cathedral fa-

çade. From here the view is total and its effect is such to convey a deep religion feeling. To this feeling a sense of bewilderment is added as we stand before the vastness and profundity of the place, as though it contained all existing architectural and sculptural works, as if not the hand of man but a divine will had aimed at creating what we are admiring. If we place ourselves in the middle of the nave, at the inner wall of the cathedral, our attention will be drawn to the long line of the imposing granite colonnades, which are almost all antique and have capitals in Corinthian style. Then the women's gallery with little loggias located above the nave, the rich, highly decorated lacunar ceiling and the ample, profound, terminal apse whereon Christ on this throne contrasts, will complete our admiration.

In brief everything including the play of the minor colonnades, the black and white panels, which line the walls, contributes to impart vivacity and movement to the gradiose realization of the temple.

The Pulpit of the Cathedral

We are before a work of rare richness if not one of the greatest masterpieces of art. In this work the plasticity of the representation seems animated of sensibility and tension that's nearly dramatic.

Nicola Pisano, father of Giovanni, in his Pulpit in the Baptistry, for instance, expresses himself with a religious gravity that is possible to note in works of the Romanesque period. His son Giovanni in his work in the Cathedral, which we are now dealing with, has on the contrary completely renounced to this precise and calculated cold reproduction, giving breath to a vehement vivacity and to a deep human sense which comes to light from his figures.

The pulpit with its hexagonal base, a work by Giovanni Pisano (1302-1310), is located near the first pillar of the vault. In the year 1599 it was dismantled and was rebuilt only in the year 1926. It rests on eleven columnar supports that in turn rest respectively on lions and on pedestals. Other supports are represented by the statues of St. Michael, Hercules, the Evangelists supporting Christ and «The four Cardinal virtues» which, in turn, support the Church. The central support represents «The Arts of the Trivium and Quadrivium». The capitals of the supports are sculptured with figures of Sibyls. In the lateral corbels there are Evangelists and Prophets. A cornice separates the above illustrated portion from the panels composing the upper portion of the pulpit and the figures of Prophets and Saints that are located between the panels.

In the panels the events proceeding and following Christ's birth are dramatically represented. They are:

1) Annunciation - Visitation - Birth of St. John the Baptist.

2) Birth of Jesus Christ.

3) The Wise Kings.

4) Presentation to the temple and the flight into Egypt.

5) The slaughter of the innocents.

6) The kiss of Judas - The arrest of Christ - The scourging of Christ.

7) The Crucifixion.

8) The chosen ones.

9) The reprobates.

On the left: **Pulpit, main altar and apse;** *on the right:* **the Pulpit by Giovanni Pisano (1302-1310).**

54

In Italia:
Agrigento
Ancona
Avellino
Bari
Bologna
Caserta
Catania
Firenze
Genova
Ischia
La Spezia
Messina
Milano Milano 2
Milano Milanofiori
Milano President
Milano Touring
Napoli
Palermo
Ravenna
Roma Leonardo Da Vinci
Roma Vittorio Veneto
Roma Midas
Salerno
Siena
Siracusa
Taormina
Torino Ambasciatori
Torino Ligure
Torino Principi di Piemonte
Trieste

In Belgio:
Bruxelles
in Francia:
Parigi
in Olanda:
Amsterdam

JOLLY ◉ HOTEL

53100 SIENA

Piazza La Lizza
Tel.: 0577/288448 (Pbx 6 linee)
Telex: 573345 JOLLSI I
Telegrammi: JOLLYOTEL
Telefax: 41272

Virgin with Child.

St. Agnes.

Virgin with Child

The Virgin with Child was completed by Antonio Sogliani (1492-1544). The artwork reflects the Tuscany style. In the performance of this artwork he chose the Raffaellean theme enhancing the gentleness and refinement typical of the great master, Raffaello Sanzio.

St. Agnes

The artwork is of Andrea del Sarto. It is one of the most famous artworks conserved at the Cathedral. In this piece of art are accentuated all the pictorial tendencies of the first Renaissance: design, color, atmosphere. The artist is a careful observer of the Leonardian style. He succeeds to carry into his paintings a personal sign of perfection from the technical-chromatic point of view.

The Apse

The famous mosaic depicting «The Redeemer between the Virgin Mary and St. John», begun by Francesco De Simone and finished by Cimabue.

The lamp of Galileo

Is at the centre of the church. It is a bronze chandelier commonly called the «Lamp of Galileo» following a popular tradition, according to which the great citizen of Pisa Galileo Galilei on observing the obscillations of the pendant, established the isochronism of the obscillations of the pendulum. However, the fact remains that this chandelier is a fine work realized from a model of B. Lorenzi in the year 1587.

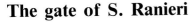
The gate of St. Ranieri, the main altar with the apse and the
lamp of Galileo Galilei.

The gate of S. Ranieri

This gate, with its bronze pillars built by
BONANNO PISANO is a masterpiece of art that
shows traces of Hellenistic and Byzantine influences. It was built in the year 1180, and made
up of 24 panels whereon are represented the
«History of the Redeemer's life». On the outside
of the gate, there is a lunette with «the Madonna, the Infant and two Angels», work relief of
Andrea di Francesco Guardi.

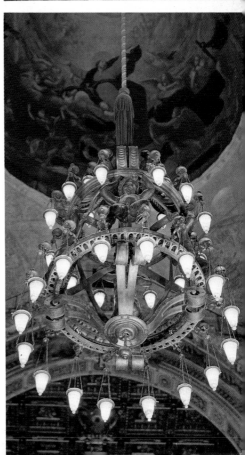

57

THE BAPTISTRY

It is located in front of the cathedral façade. The construction of this great building began in the year 1153 under the guide of architect DIOTISALVI, as stated on an epigraph situated inside the monument on a pillar. Hence it was the second monument to rise in the square, given that the works of the church belltower (or Leaning Tower) began many years later, i.e. in the year 1174. Also in the case of the Baptistry its construction progressed as for the other monuments of the «Piazza dei Miracoli», i.e. from the beginning to the end of the works many years lapsed, due to interruptions of different causes. In fact, only at the end of the 14th century was the work terminated.

The Baptistry has a circular base, three orders (or storeys) and from the third order (or Tambour) rises the dome. The height of this imposing monument is 55 mts, with a diameter of 35.50 mts. It has four gates, the principal of which opens towards the façade of the Cathedral. In spite of its gigantic mass, its aspect is refined by a multiple series of ornaments in Gothic style.

The first storey is with blind arcades like the Leaning Tower and the Cathedral but with the variation that in this work windows have single apertures. The second order or storey presents an open gallery surmounted by ornamental aedicules with «busts». There are, furthermore, cusps on which statues of Nicola PISANO and his school rest. Most sculptures which, as we have said, are both in the niches and on the cusps of this second storey, are substituted by copies, while the originals are at the Museum of the «Opera del Duomo». Other cusps rise magnificently, between the aedicules and minor cusps,

extending beyond the second order or storey, up to the third order (or tambour), at the same height of the extremely beautiful mullioned windows which are the main ornament of this storey. Above the third order or storey rises the dome whereon are other windows between the ribs.

Interior of the Baptistry

On entering the baptistry, the immensity of the building is even more convincing than from outside. Here, in fact, we obtain an immediate sense of the proportions. We have said that the height is 55 mts and the diameter 35.50 mts: bare values, but from the inside, at this moment, the height and amplitude have another meaning, so penetrating as to cause admiration and dismay. We are, in fact, under the huge vault of the dome and in front of a grandiose annular nave lighted almost with discretion by the numerous windows distributed all around. We are facing an imposing and high colonnade alternated with pillars that, detached from the wall, delimitate a nave. Above is a very wide gallery with high arcades well lighted by windows.

Below: **an aerial view of the monuments in the Cathedral Square;** *right:* **the Baptistry (1174-1300).**

Baptistry Fountain

Our attention will be very soon drawn by the Font and the Pulpit. The font is located in the middle of the temple on three steps. It is a work of the 13th century by GUIDO BIGARELLI. The big octagonal basin, which incorporates other four smaller basins, was realized for baptism by immersion. In the middle of the basin there is a beautiful statue of the Baptist, a work by ITALO GRISELLI. The font is enriched with eight faces decorated by central rose-windows and by geometrical marble decorations. The altar, located close to the font, is composed of six panels with marble inlays and rose-windows. It is surrounded by inlaid seats of the 17th century. Looking towards the altar we can appreciate a cosmati-floor from the 14th century.

The Pulpit of the Baptistry

This is a great work of the year 1260 by NICOLA PISANO. The artist, for realizing the last panel of this opera, was helped by his still very young son Giovanni and by ARNOLFO DI CAMBIO, both of whom later cooperated with him in realizing the pulpit for the cathedral of Siena. The pulpit of the baptistry has a hexagonal base supported by seven columns, three of which rest on supporting lions on the sides. The central column rests on a base depicting sculptured animals and human figures. This work evidently reveals a marked inspiration of the artist to the romanesque art of this time and a need to express himself with a composed piety. Nevertheless it is not lacking in poetry even though it doesn't seem to exhalt a human sense of inspiration, which on the other hand his son Giovanni desired and later manifested in the grandiose realization of the pulpit of the cathedral.

In the pendentives of the little arches there are figures of «Prophets». In the pillars of the corners are depicted: «Faith», «Charity», «Force», «Humility», «Fidelity» and «Innocence». In the panels there are represented:

1) The Nativity and Announcement to the Shepherds.
2) The Adoration of the Wise Kings.
3) The Presentation to the Temple.
4) The Crucifixion.
5) The last Judgement.

In the baptistry, if one asks the attendants, it is interesting to hear the echo. On the inside for instance, a melody reechoes many times through the ample vault and it gives the impression of hearing a strange, harmonious and multitoned big organ.

Below: **Baptismal Font, by G. Da Como (1200);** *right:* **the Pulpit, made by Nicola Pisano in 1260.**

THE LEANING TOWER

This is the monument that, among the others of the «Piazza dei Miracoli» stirs the imagination of practically everybody, from the old to the young. Firstly we would like to give you some information and events regarding its long history.

The construction of this imposing mass was started in the year 1174 by BONANNO PISANO. When the tower reached its third storey operations ceased because it had started sinking into the ground. The tower remained thus for 90 years. It was completed by GIOVANNI DI SIMONE. TOMMASO, son of ANDREA PISANO, crowned the tower with the belfry in the middle of the 14th century.

The top of the Leaning Tower can be reached by mounting the 294 steps which rise in the form of a spiral on the inner side of the tower walls.

The tower is 55.863 mts high.

The inside diameter at the base is 7.368 mts.

The outer diameter at the base is 15.484 mts.

The inclination is 4.551 mts.

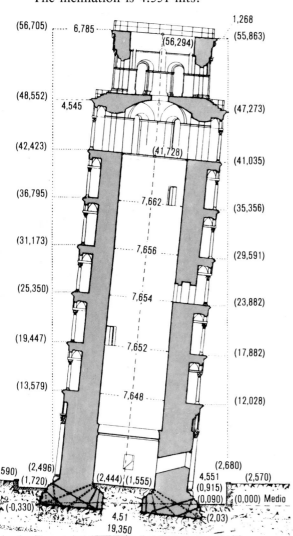

There are 8 storeys.

It is supported by foundations of about 3 mts.

The Tower weighs about 14,500 tons.

In the belfry there are 7 bells each one of them corresponding to a note of the musical scale.

The oldest bell is that named «Pasquareccia» which rang to announce that the Earl Ugolino della Gherardesca, sentenced for treachery, was starving to death together with his sons and nephews in the tower of Piazza delle Sette Vie (today Piazza dei Cavalieri). On the top of the tower GALILEO GALILEI carried out famous experiments regarding the effects of gravity. From the top we can enjoy a vast view, that starting from the Pisan Mountains, the mountains of Garfagnana and the Apuan Alps slopes down towards us, demonstrating the great extent of the whole fertile plain, which, before reaching the sea, meets the grandiose and extensive forest regions of Migliarino and S. Rossore.

Art of the Tower

The very famous work is in Romanesque style, and as already mentioned dates back to the year 1174. Cylindrical in shape it shows externally six open galleries. A cornice separates these galleries from one another and each presents a series of small arches fitted on the capitals of the slender columns. At the base there is a series of big blind arcades with a number of geometrical decorations. In the belfry there is the same design of arcades as that of the base, with the difference that here, there are, apart from the reduced proportions, apertures or doors for the housing of the bells.

The Campanile (Bell Tower) or Leaning Tower, by Bonanno Pisano (1174

Above - from left to right: **the Roman column at the base of the Leaning Tower; suggestive shots of the Tower;** *below:* **a bas-relief situated at the base of the Tower. It records the date of the beginning of the construction works.**

The Leaning Tower and the Cathedral Apse. ▶

Although stately, this monument is not lacking in elegance and lightness due to this dense location of arcades and open galleries between one storey and another.

Although it can be considered a real masterpiece of architecture, this monument is mostly famous for its strong inclination. Regarding this inclination it can be safely stated that is undoubtedly due to a sinking of the ground right from the time of its construction. Therefore, for those who desire to imagine that great tower was intentionally built inclined, this assumption is entirely without foundation. Unfortunately, even today the great mass continues to sink even if very slowly. It is a question of about 1 mm. every year. Since nobody can say with matematical security that this sinking effect will continue in the future at the present yearly rate, remedies by means of adequate measures, based on scientific studies and projects, are under consideration. In the meantime supervision of the effect with instruments of very high precision is continuously being carried out.

THE MONUMENTAL CEMETERY

Coming out of the baptistry and looking once more at the majestic façade of the cathedral on we will see to the left the churchyard which presents its long marble walls in the form of a rectangle. These boundary walls are composed of blind arcades on pilasters similar to those of the cathedral, tower and the baptistry just visited. In these walls there are two entrances in the arcades. The main gate is on the right to the cathedral, over which a Gothic three-cusped tabernacle with «Madonna and Saints» stands out. It is a work of the school of Giovanni Pisano.

Before passing over to the description of other things, it is to be said that the churchyard is a work that dates back to about the end of the 13th century and was started by GIOVANNI DI SIMONE. Centuries passed before it was ultimated, just as for the other monuments of the square.

It is said that the archbishop Ubaldo de' Lanfranchi, in 1200, brought earth from the Golgotha Mountain with galleys coming back from a crusade, because it seemed that this earth was capable of reducing a body into a skeleton within twenty-four hours. When Giovanni di Simone started the works the churchyard already existed. In fact, the aim of this monumental work as started by him was to gather within a limited area in an orderly and dignified manner all the graves scattered around the cathedral and at the same time to leave space for others in the future on the basis of the deeply rooted tradition of the noble families of Pisa of that time.

Later, ancient sculptures, sepulchral monuments, works of art scattered around the city, were gathered inside the churchyard. Sarcofagi of famous men lined the walls, that were frescoed by different, great artists. All this rendered the «Camposanto Monumentale» (Monumental churchyard) of Pisa progressively one of the greatest and richest galleries of medieval painting and sculpture, besides representing a great masterpiece of architecture. During the 2nd World War this enormous artistic and cultural patrimony suffered severe damages and losses during the bombing raid of the 27th July 1944. The roof caught fire melting the lead-plates covering the roof, and the molten lead dropped down on the works of art. Today many of these works have been restored but have not been situated in their original places but temporarily scattered here and there around the walls. Others are located in appropriate rooms.

The tabernacle

The especially linear and unitary style of this immense construction, the Monumental Cemetery, is interrupted only by the gracious gothic decoration of the Tabernacle. The Virgin Enthroned with the four saints and a believer kneeling in an act of devotion are located within its graceful interior. This construction was completed during the second half of the 14th century. It is presumed to be designed by a possible disciple of Giovanni Pisano since it tends to remind one of the inimitable grace of the great master.

The Churchyard from Inside

On entering the churchyard ones attention is immediately drawn to the great colonnade that opens out on an inner lawn with its great, round arcades. These latter are each adorned by four-apertured small windows with fine, plurilobed, little arches.

However, looking around at the walls of the colonnade and seeing only the remains of frescoes we cannot but feel a deep sorrow in thinking what our eyes could have admired today if the rage of the 2nd World War had saved this monumental spot with everything in its place. Saddened by this thought now it remains to content oneself by imagining the precious art gallery as it was before the war and looking for the remaining works, removed to be restored. For some of these pieces a special room has been arranged: the «Triumph of Death», «The Last Judgement» and «The Anchorets». Concerning the ruddle-works, which are the preparatory sketches for frescoes, brought to light when the same frescoes were detached from the wall for restauration, it is to be said that they are of great interest.

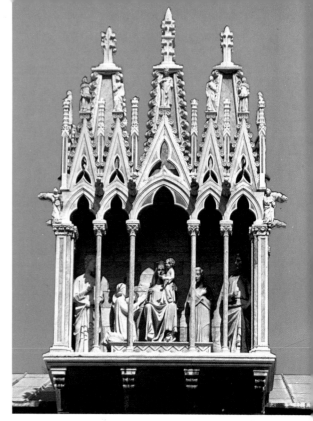

Tabernacle in the Cemetery.

Interior of the Cemetery.

Above: **North wall in wich a number of Roman and Greecian sarcophagi are placed. The most famous of them (*picture below*) was the tomb of Beatrice of Canossa, mother of countess Mathilda, and is sculptured with the tale of Hippolytus and Phaedra (II century).**

QVAMVIS PECCATRIX SVM DOMNA VOCATA BEATRIX
IN TVMVLO MISSA IACEO QVAE COMITISSA.
A.D.M.LXXVI.

The salon of the Triumph of Death

In this salon are jealously guarded and gathered frescoes by the «Master of the Triumph of Death», including the Triumph of Death, the Universal Judgment, Hell and the History of the Anchorets, the Crucifixion and the Ascension.

In the art world, even today, there is energetic discussion concerning the authorship of this large cycle of frescoes. The hypotheses advanced mention the names of Orcagna, Pietro Lorenzetti, Francesco Traini, Vitale da Bologna and Buonamico di Buffalmacco.

THE MUSEUM OF THE CATHEDRAL VESTRY BOARD

The museum contains works which used to adorn the monuments of the Piazza dei Miracoli and which, mainly for safety reasons, had been moved to the warehouses of the Cathedral Vestry Board. It was set up in 1986 in a specially restored building, between Piazza dell'Arcivescovado and Piazza del Duomo, which had been originally designed as a capitular seat (13th century) and then turned into an enclosure monastery. The exhibition takes up rooms on two different floors and the visit is made pleasant by the variety of works displayed and by an exceptionally good set of captions.

On the ground floor the following works are of particular value: the wooden crucifix by Borgognone; the bronze hippogryph; the Citharoedus David; the Madonnas by Giovanni Pisano, particularly the so-called «Madonna del colloquio» and the ivory small statue; the sculptures by Tino di Camaino, by Nino and Tommaso Pisano, by Andrea Guardi, etc.; the precious objects forming the «Treasure», with the crucifix by Giovanni Pisano, the Limoges caskets and the «Cathedral's belt»; the silverware of the Cathedral sacristy. On the upper floor: large paintings on canvas; some of the Cathedral's old fittings together with some precious wooden marquetries; miniated parchments; sacred vestments; printings of the 19th century representing the frescoes of the Camposanto and a rich archeological collection with Roman, Etruscan and Egyptian objects.

These works flow before visitors along the museum path, thus reminding them of the events which accompanied the life of the monuments and of the town of Pisa: the Islamic influences, the sculptures of the 14th century, the spiritual inheritance of the ancient Rome.

1) Entrance to the Museum. 2) Busts lined up in the interior of the cloister portico). 3) Our Lady with Child and ivory work by G. Pisano. 4) Julius Caesar's head. 5) «Alcove» hall. 6) Hall with a sculpture by G. Pisano. 7) Our Lady with Child known as the «Madonna of the Talk». 8) John the Baptist, by G. Pisano.

70

3

5

6

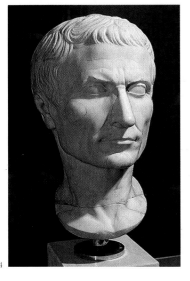

4

7

8

THE MUSEUM OF THE SINOPIES

Entrance to the Museum.

The museum has been set up in a time-battered hospital pavilion, restored in 1979, which was part of a building erected in 1257 by Giovanni di Simone, the same architect who, later on, would build the Monumental Cemetery. The historical link between these two constructions was to manifest itself again after centuries. In 1944 the Cemetery was devastated by a fire during which the works of art preserved in its rooms and, above all, the famous fresco cycle painted on its walls, were badly damaged. The following peeling off of the damaged frescoes, which was a necessary stage of the restoration, has brought to light the preparatory sketches which had been hidden by the plaster. The discovery of the sinopies, whose name comes from the Turkish town of Sinope which supplied the earth used as colouring matter to paint them, has been a major artistic event, both because these works had remained unseen up to that time and because, thanks to the freshness of their execution, they sometimes are more valuable than the cor-

responding frescoes. The fifty or so sketches displayed in the museum were painted on the walls of the Camposanto in the 14th and 15th century and represent undoubtedly the biggest collection of its kind. The artists are those considered as the authors of the Camposanto frescoes: Buonamico di Buffalmacco, Francesco Traini, Antonio Veneziano, Spinello Aretino, Taddeo Gaddi, Piero di Puccio and Benozzo Gozzoli.

On the upper floors visitors walk on modern modular structures; photographic reproductions on panels of the most important frescoes allow comparisons which reveal the author's insights and changes of mind during the tormenting phases of the thinking up and execution of the paintings.

Finally, it is advisable to visit the Monumental Cemetery in order to complete the information acquired in the Museum of the Sinopies.

Museum opening times:
9 to 12.30 a.m. - 3 to 7 p.m. during the summer; 9 to 12.30 a.m. - 3 to 4.30 p.m. during the winter. The change from the summer to the winter opening times occurs gradually, following the length of daylight.

Tales of Agar and Abraham: Abraham.

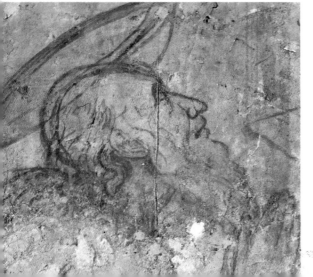

Opposite, from above: **1) The Last Judgement: Angels. 2) The last Judgement: Hell with the figure of Lucifer. 3) Tales of the Anchorites: lower part. 4) Adoration of the Magi: one of the Kings**

1

2

3

4

HORSEMEN'S SQUARE

After the «Piazza dei Miracoli» we would suggest to start the visit of the town from the «Piazza dei Cavalieri», not only because it is the most important and beautiful square, after that of the cathedral, but also because it is nearby. Leaving the cathedral and entering the old Via S. Maria we turn later down Via dei Mille and come out at Piazza dei Cavalieri. We find here a group of buildings that surround it irregularly but at the same time with an extraordinary harmony. We notice at once the Palace of the Knights'Caravan (after which the square is named) where now the Superior Normal College seats. Beyond that, we see the National Church of St. Stephen of the Knights. The Clock Palace is on the left of the entrance of the Via dei Mille. On the opposite side of the Clock Palace, there is the Palace of Puteano College and the Council Palace of the Order of St. Stephen. The fountain located in the square is a work of the year 1596 by P. Francavilla. In proximity to it is the statue of Cosimo the 1st de' Medici, who founded the Order of the Knights of St. Stephen.

NATIONAL CHURCH OF ST. STEPHEN OF THE KNIGHTS

This is a work from the 16th century by Vasari who, later, also built the bell-tower in 1572. The church presents a marble façade by Don Giovanni de' Medici (1606) with a single portal in the middle, above which is the Emblem of the Knights Order. Flanking the sides of the church are two wings that were once used as dressing-rooms for the knights of the order of St. Stephen. These are later transformed into two aisles of the church by Pier Francesco Silvani.

The inside - It has an only nave with an extremely beautiful wooden inlaid ceiling. In each of the six partitions, into which it is divided, is a painting representing «The glory of the knights». These works are by C. Allori, Empoli, Ligozzi and Cigoli.

On entering the church we can admire two precious holy water founts by Vasari while, on the right and left hand wall, we see, high between the windows, four ship lanterns. These same walls are hung with tapestry and flags captured from the Turks. In this church there are also figureheads of ships of St. Stephen's Order. Still on

Piazza dei Cavalieri: the Secondary School of the Cavalieri (Knights) and the Church of St. Stephen of the Cavalieri.

Interior of the Church of St. Stephen of the Knights.

the wall we see four distempers (two on each side) representing «Episodes of St. Stephen Life», works by Vasari, Empoli, Allori and Ligozzi. To be noted is also the small but precious marble pulpit of the year 1627 by C. Fancelli. The walls of the church have four doors — two on both sides — which open into the two aisles that, as previously mentioned, were used as dressing-rooms for the Knights of St. Stephen.

In the right aisle at the first altar we see the «Lapidation of St. Stephen» by G. Vasari. At the second altar there is a crucifix by Tacca. In the left aisle at the first altar, near the exit of the church, there is «The miracle of the loaves and fishes» by Buti; at the second altar the «Nativity of Jesus» a work by Bronzino.

At the high altar there is the sarcophag of St. Stephen Pope (P.F. Silvani and Giovan Battista Foggini, 1700). Behind the altar a gilt bronze bust of «St. Lussorio» of Donatello is preserved under a glass-bell.

Of all the palaces which surround the square let us dwell a little upon that, that today is the seat of the Normal Superior School, a renovation by Vasari — 16th century — of the old Palace of the Elders of the Pisan Republic. This building was appointed by Cosimo the 1st de' Medici to receive the military order of knight of St. Stephen, hence it was also called «Palace of the Caravan». Remarkable is the originality of the building, its slight curvature with a graffito-decorated façade, a series of busts of the Grand Dukes of Tuscany of that time at the second storey and in the middle, above a balcony, the escutcheon of the Medici family.

Now we are in front of the original Palace of the Clock that is a successful architectural utilization of two ancient towers constructed from designs of Vasari, that is the tower of Gualandi (or Gherardesca) with the other of the TOWN-JAIL or Torre delle Sette Vie. In the tower of Gualandi imprisoned for treachery together with sons and nephews Count Ugolino starved to death. Count Ugolino was at that time Podestà of the town and the Marine Republic of Pisa had just suffered a clamorous defeat on the sea by the Republic of Genoa in the very famous battle of Meloria (1284).

Of minor touristic interest are the Palace Puteano of the 17th century and the Palace of the Council of the Order (Francavilla 1603), then seat of the Law-Court of St. Stephens'Order and today seat of the Superior School for applied sciences «A. Pacinotti».

CHURCH OF SANTA MARIA DELLA SPINA

This jewel of Gothic art of Pisan-style is located on the Lungarno Gambacorti. Initially it was an oratory at the extreme limit of the Arno River. After it was enlarged by Lupo Capomaestro in 1323 and named Chiesa della Spina (church of the thorn) because it preserves one of the thorns of the Christ crown. In the year 1871,

after about five hundred years, the church was dismantled piece by piece and rebuilt in a safer location away from the river waters that had badly damaged it. This very beautiful small church is covered with an extremely rich marble decorations of gentle contrasting colours and a suggestive series of cusps and pinnacles. In the façade with three cusps there are two wooden, inlaid gates. A very fine «Madonna with Infant and Angels» of G. DI BALDUCCIO is located in an aedicule in the centre. Other aedicules are located above it with statues of the School of Giovanni Pisano. Also of the school of Giovanni Pisano are the other aedicules to the right of the church with statues of the Redeemer and of the Apostles, while the statues located on the spires of the aedicules of this side are a work of Nino Pisano and his pupils.

The inside is with a nave divided by three arcades on pillars and by the presbitery. Here are works of Tommaso, son of Andrea Pisano, of the Madonna with Infant and statue of St. Peter and St. John the Baptist. The «Madonna weaning her Child» of Nino Pisano together with the bas-reliefs of A. F. Guardi are no longer preserved in this church but in the National Museum; they are precious works of art.

Above: **The Church of St. Mary of the Thorn.** *On the left*: **The Solferino Bridge over the Arno.**

76

NATIONAL MUSEUM OF ST. MATTHEW

The National Museum of Pisa can be rightly considered one of the most important in Europe especially for its collection of medieval and Renaissance paintings. Many of the sculptures in wood, stone or marble are certainly unique.

If at the beginning the aim of this gallery was to collect the works of the local art of the said flourishing period, it is to be considered that this aim was largely surpassed, because neither their seat can be considered definitive (after the various moves of the works collected piece by piece through the centuries), nor can the room be considered sufficient because of the continuous affluence of works, while others are removed for re-housing in their original places. The Museum has today its seat in an architectural complex that was initially a Benedictine nunnery, then respectively town-jail and military barraks. As a consequence of all this, it progressively lose its original structure and in 1945 new restoration works were started for the building to be able to receive the works of art in the year 1949.

The entrance of the St. Matthew Museum.

The Cloister of the Monastery of St. Matthew.

St. Paul,
by Masaccio
(1429)

Our Lady of the Milk, by Nino Pisano (1300).

Our Lady with Child and Saints,
by Simone Martini.

SIENA

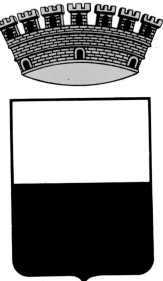

SIENA
Historic notes

It would seem that the foundation of Siena can be attributed to no less than the sons of one of the founders of Rome: Remus. On the death of their father, it seems that the two boys, Aschius and Senus, distrustful of their uncle Romulus, decided to flee from Rome. But they were poor and did not even have a horse on which to escape. They entreated Apollo to help them, promising to erect a temple to him in exchange. Their request was granted: two horses, one white and one black, appeared seemingly from nowhere. The boys mounted the two fiery steeds which galloped away without stopping until they had covered sone 230 kilometres. When they did stop, the boys dismounted and the first thing they did was to erect the temple. Then they thought of a house for themselves. And so Siena was born.

Who knows if this is really what happened; it is certain, however, that the name of the city is very similar to the name of one of Remus's sons. Some think, less romantically, that the name Siena is derived from the Senonian Gauls, or Senese, who were the founders. But the fact that the city's coat of arms includes a she-wolf leads us to think that the Sienese prefer to consider themselves as Remus's heirs.

A rapid excursion into Siena's history: a Roman colony, it was converted to Christianity towards the end of the fourth century. It underwent sieges and invasions and, in the XI century, after being under the rule of the Carolingians, passed to the Bishops under whom it remained for less than 100 years when the Consuls gained the upper hand, giving the city new life. Siena, favouring the Ghibellines, knew great splendour in that period, but being considered a dangerous rival of the Guelph supporter, Florence, became its untamed rival. In 1253, Florence gained the advantage and compelled its rival to a forced peace with drastic results: Sienese territories were taken away from the mother-city. Siena conformed and rebuilt its image. But the conflict was not over; Florence once more tried to gain the upper hand and, in spite of two victories beneath its walls and at Montaperti, Siena with its allies Pisa, Pistoia and Arezzo, was defeated in 1296.

From then on, relationships with Florence changed and Siena, governed by the «Nine» (representatives of a like number of families), regained its splendour. It again underwent various rules, plagues, wars and outrages, never surrendering but always reacting with an untamed spirit until 1553 when it was forced to give in to the siege of Germans and Spaniards, finishing under the rule of Cosimo de' Medici in 1559. It remained under the Medicis for a long period until, with the rest of Tuscany, it passed to the House of Lorena.

The Risorgimento witnessed Siena in the foreground and, in 1859, it was the first city of the region to attach itself to the Kingdom of Italy. Splendid monuments and art treasures bear witness to the culture and the life of the city: the Palazzo Pubblico (Town Hall), built between 1297 and 1310 with the Torre del Mangia (bell tower) (1348); the Fonte Gaia (Fontain of Yoy) (1419); the Duomo and Baptistry (1100-1376); the Merchant's House; the monumental and intact walls (seven kilometres long) with their gates: on one of these, Porta Camollia, is written the famous phrase «Cor mangis tibi Sena pandit» or «Siena opens an even greater heart to you» (than this gate); St. Dominic's Church; the Chigi-Saracini Palace; Fontebranda; the St. Barbara fortress; the house of St. Catherine, etc.

As well as the Patron Saint of Italy, Siena is also the birthplace of many famous people such as the sculptor Jacopo della Quercia, the painters Duccio di Boninsegna, Pietro Lorenzetti and Simone Martini, the painter and architect Baldassarre Peruzzi and the novelist Federico Tozzi, etc.

Piazza del Campo with its highly original fan shaped form at the base of which is the Town Hall with its elegant Torre del Mangia

PIAZZA DEL CAMPO

This square, which has always been the heart of the city, has a shape which is unique throughout the world. Situated at the confluence of the three hills on which Siena stands, it has an original scollop or fan shape, emphasized by the caracteristic rosy colour of its stone flooring. Subdivided into nine «segments» which branch out in front of the Palazzo Pubblico and which are a reference to the Rule of the Nine, it is surrounded by flagstones which are almost a frame for the square and by a series of splendid palaces. Standing under the Torre del Mangia with one's back to it, on the right we have Palazzo Piccolomini, built in the XV century and a work which was perhaps based on a plan by Bernardo Rossellini. Today it houses the State Archives, containing precious documents and the famous «tavolette» (wooden tablets) which protected the books of the an-

cient Rule and which were decorated by leading Sienese artists. Next to this is Palazzo Chigi-Zondadari which has undergone various rearrangements with respect to the original plan. Then Palazzo Sansedoni, begun at the beginning of the XIII century. The tower was originally much higher. Then we have the rear part

The Sansedoni Palace surmounted by a rhomb-shaped tower, built in 1216 and enlarged in 1339

Fonte Gaia (Fountain of Joy), the work of Jacopo di Pietro (Della Quercia) made between 1409-1419

of the Merchant's House, of the early XV century, the original plan of which is attributed to Sano di Matteo, while the side which faces the square designed by Niccolò dei Cori.

Among the many jewels of the Piazza del Campo, particular mention is due to the Fonte Gaia (Fountain of Joy), situated at the other head of the square, in front of the Palazzo Pubblico, and the work of Jacopo della Quercia. Built at

The Chapel of the Piazza, situated at the base of the Town Hall

the beginning of the XV century, it has been supplied by an aqueduct since the middle of the XIV century and owes its name to the joy which reigned in the days in which it was inaugurated. The statues which adorn it are not the original ones; for fear that they would deteriorate even further, the originals have been removed to the Palazzo Pubblico, leaving in their place the copies made last century by Tito Sarrocchi. They represent, in order from left to right, the creation of Adam, Wisdom, Hope, Strength, Prudence, an angel, the Madonna with Child, another angel, Justice, Charity, Temperance, Faith, and the banishment from the Garden of Eden.

The Cappella di Piazza (Chapel of the Square) is also of great artistic interest. Built in the XIV century to commemorate the end of a plague, it is decorated by a series of statues of saints placed in the pillars. The prized fresco of Sodoma has unfortunately been damaged over the years by the elements.

But the real jewel is the Palazzo Pubblico which was begun in the second half of the XIII century. Built in the Tuscan Gothic style, it was based on a plan by Agostino di Giovanni and Angelo di Ventura. At present it is the seat of the Town Hall and also houses several remarkable works of art. At its side is the Torre del Mangia, 88 metres high, built in the XIV century by Minuccio an Francesco di Rinaldo. It owes its name to its first bell-ringer, Mangiaguadagni or «Mangia».

View of the Town Hall ▶

ĀNO · DŃI · MCCC · XXVIII

SALA DEL MAPPAMONDO

Its name is derived from the huge map depicting the Siennese territory, the work of Ambrogio Lorenzetti (1300). *Above:* Guidoriccio da Fogliano, a masterpiece by Simone Martini (1315); *left:* Sala del Mappamondo, today the home of the Town Museum; *right:* the «Maestà» (1315), by Simone Martini depicting the Madonna on a Throne among Angels and Saints

Piazza del Campo during the «Palio»

The «Mossa», the start of the «Palio»

IL PALIO

To talk of the Piazza del Campo without mentioning the Palio is impossible. It is in fact here that twice a year, on July 2nd and August 16th, the ancient tournament of horses between the contrade (parishes) is held. Ten of the seventeen contrade into which the city is divided are chosen at random. These bear the names of Aquila, Chiocciola, Onda, Pantera, Selva, Tartuca, Civetta, Leocorna, Nicchio, Valdimonte, Torre, Bruco, Drago, Giraffa, Istrice, Lupa e Oca. And every year, tend of thousands of spectators watch this stupendous scenographic dispute. The Palio is not, however, merely a show: it is the very essence of the city, which on these dates parades the ancient passions which bore witness to its fighting and untamed spirit. The great festival begins some days before the dispute with the drawing of the horses, which are then blessed together with their jockeys in the respective churches of each parish on the day of the Palio. In the morning of the race, mass is celebrated in the Cappella di Piazza while the parish standards and the Palio itself are blessed in the church of Santa Maria di Provenzano on July 2nd and in the Cathedral on August 16th. In the afternoon the historic parade takes place, opened by the mace-bearers of the Commune and followed by the centurions, the representatives of the ten parishes drawn for the Palio, those of the excluded parishes and finally the Carroccio (chariot) on which the Palio (prize) is placed. While the bell in the Torre del Mangia tolls, the solemn moment of the race takes place. It lasts only a minute, the time necessary for the horses to run three times round the square with their jockeys riding bareback and the crowd shouting encourangement. Then the triumph of the winners.

The seat of the contrada of the Goose (Oca)

The Palio Procession   The Race

THE DUOMO

More than two centuries were needed to complete the construction of magnificent Sienese churc. Begun in around 1150, it was not finished until 1376. Its foundations stand on an ancient pagan temple and, precisely because it was constructed over such a long period, it bears traces of various styles: Romanesque, Gothic, ornate Gothic. The lower part of the beautiful façade in pink Siena stone and green Prato stone is the work of Giovanni Pisano while the upper part is that of Giovanni de Cecco. The three spires contain mosaics by Castellani, of the last century. Under the central spire is a large rose-window with scenes from the Last Supper and around this are the busts of the four Evangelists and of 36 Patriarchs and Prophets. The dome has a hexagonally shaped base. The precious paving, uncovered only from August 15th to September 15th, is one of its rarest attributes. It consists of 56 pictures and was the work of about forty artists among whom were Matteo di Giovanni, Urbano da Cortona, Antonio Federighi, Domenico Beccafumi, Domenico di Bartolo, etc. Among the works of particular note are the statues of Bernini, a prized stained glass window designed by Duccio di Boninsegna, numerous works by Jacopo della Quercia and other famous works, among which is Nicola Pisano's wonderful pulpit. Supported by nine columns of granite, porphyry and marble (a central one and the others to hold up the octagonal base), the upper part is divided into various panels, separated by statues of Saints and Prophets. The façades represent the Nativity, the Adoration of the Magi, the Presentation at the Temple, the Massacre of the Innocents, the Crucifixion, the Final Judgement of the Bad and the Final Judgement of the Good. The eighth façades is that of the «opening» of the access stairway.

Below: the Cathedral, one of the most prestigious and richest in Europe; *right:* the façade of the Cathedral, the lower section of which was made by Giovanni Pisano with the upper area, divided into two sections by a large cornice, by Giovanni di Cecco

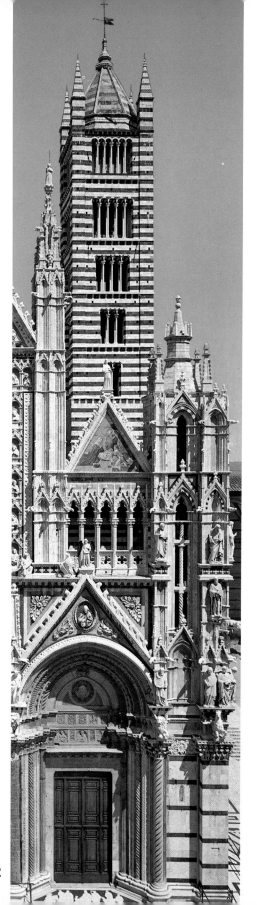

The Cathedral. *Left:* The Bell Tower, built in 1313, to a design by Agostino di Giovanni and Agnolo di Ventura with marble decorations forming horizontal black and white strips in imitation of the colours inside the church. It has six windows progressing from the single-lighted one towards the base, to the six-lighted one towards the top, and terminating in a pyramid-shaped spire with a polygon base; *at the top:* a detail of the facade: a mosaic by Veneziano Castellani, representing the Coronation of Mary; *bottom:* interior of the Cathedral: detail of the Pulpit by Nicola Pisano showing the Crucifixion; *right:* interior of the Cathedral - the Pulpit by Nicola Pisano (1268)

SAN GIMIGNANO

The attraction of San Gimignano lies in the charm of its 14 towers — originally there were 72 — that soar above the town proper, the unmistakable landmarks uniquely distinguishing the medieval city.

Dominating the Elsa valley (settled by the Etruscans) with its olive groves and vineyards from its hilltop vantage, the town was originally founded on farming and trade along the ancient Via Francigena. With the rise of the communes, 12th-13th centuries, San Gimignano's main monuments begin to take form and project skyward above the same throughfare. This era also marks the height of the town's expansion with the addition of the San Matteo and San Giovanni districts beside the older fortified nucleus and the erection round them of the walls in the late 13th century (most of these walls are still preserved). Once encircled, the old city was to remain intact, impervious to the influences of Florence and Siena, both of which ruled the town at different times, as well as those of the Renaissance and neoclassicism. Unspoiled even today, it is perhaps the most engaging example of a medieval town in all Tuscany and a genuine point of interest for any visitor.

2

95

3

4

1) S. Gimignano: scenic panorama. 2) Piazza della Cisterna with the cisterna (1273) at the centre.
3) Panorama of the Piazza del Duomo, the Palazzo del Podestà and its Torre Rognosa which dominates the villages and the wide expanse of the surrounding lowlands. 4) One of the town's charming streets. 5) Medieval tower and the Arco dei Becci.

5

94

INDEX

Tuscany, general notices . . . . pag. 2

FLORENCE

Historical notices . . . . » 4
Giotto's Bell-Tower . . . . » 5
The Piazza del Duomo . . . . » 6
The Baptistery . . . . » 12
Museum of the Opera del Duomo . . . . » 15
The Piazza della Signoria . . . . » 17
The Loggia della Signoria . . . . » 19
His Lordship's Palace . . . . » 21
The Uffizi Gallery . . . . » 23
The Old Bridge . . . . » 30
The Pitti Palace . . . . » 32
Medici Chapels . . . . » 38
Galleria dell'Accademia . . . . » 40
The «Bargello» . . . . » 42
Basilica of S. Lorenzo . . . . » 43
Basilica of S. Croce . . . . » 45
Museum of S. Marco . . . . » 46

PISA

It's history . . . . » 48
Cathedral Square . . . . » 50
The Dome . . . . » 51
The Baptistry . . . . » 58
The Leaning Tower . . . . » 62
The Monumental Cemetery . . . . » 66
The Museum of the Cathedral vestry board . . . . » 70
The Museum of the Sinopies . . . . » 72
Horsemen's Square . . . . » 74
National Church of St. Stephen of the Knights . . . . » 74
Church of Santa Maria della Spina . . . . » 75
National Museum of St. Matthew . . . . » 77

SIENA

Historic notes . . . . » 82
Piazza del Campo . . . . » 83
The Pubblic Palace . . . . » 85
Il Palio . . . . » 89
The Duomo . . . . » 90
S. Gimignano . . . . » 94

editions **ITALCARDS**
bologna - italy
Copyright by Fotometalgrafica Emiliana
All rights reserved
No part of this publication may be reproduced without prior permissione

Printed at the
Fotometalgrafica Emiliana printing press.
S. Lazzaro di Savena (Bologna)